Pruning Success

Andrew Mikolajski

HERMES
HOUSE

This edition published by Hermes House,
an imprint of Anness Publishing Limited
Hermes House, 88–89 Blackfriars Road, London SE1 8HA

A CIP catalogue record for this book is available from the British Library.

Publisher Joanna Lorenz
Editor: Valerie Ferguson
Series Designer: Larraine Shamwana
Designer: Ian Sandom
Photography: Peter Anderson,
Jonathan Buckley, John Freeman, Andrea Jones,
Marie O'Hara

The publishers would like to thank the following people for allowing
their pictures to be reproduced in this book: Peter McHoy for the pictures on page 11 (top),
page 34 (bottom right), page 37 (top), page 38 (top), page 41 (top left), page 53 (top);
Andrew Mikolajski for the picture on page 14 (top).

1 3 5 7 9 10 8 6 4 2

CONTENTS

INTRODUCTION	4
EQUIPMENT	9
GENERAL PRUNING TECHNIQUES	12
PRUNING BY PLANT TYPE	24
Roses	24
Clematis	30
Honeysuckle	34
Wisteria	35
Other Climbers	36
Wall-trained Chaenomeles	37
Wall-trained Pyracanthas	38
Ornamental Vines	39
Conifers	40
New Hedges	42
Formal Hedges	43
Informal Flowering Hedges	44
Rejuvenating a Neglected Hedge	45
Dwarf Bush Apple	46
Espalier Apple	47
Cordon Apple	48
Raspberries	49
Gooseberries	50
Black, Red & White Currants	51
Blackberries & Hybrid Berries	52
Blueberries	53
METHODS OF PRUNING CHART	54
SEASONAL PRUNING CHART	60
COMMON NAMES OF PLANTS	62
INDEX	63

Introduction

PRUNING IS A TECHNIQUE USED TO RESTRICT THE GROWTH OF PLANTS, INCREASE THE YIELD OF FLOWERS AND FRUIT AND GENERALLY KEEP PLANTS IN GOOD HEALTH. IT CAN ALSO BE USED TO ENHANCE THE DECORATIVE EFFECT OF LEAVES AND STEMS.

PRUNING CONCERNS

Amateur gardeners are often more baffled by pruning than by any other aspect of gardening; this may be partly due to conflicting advice in publications, and on television and radio programmes. Even many experienced gardeners approach the subject with caution. The main concerns are that pruning incorrectly will result in the failure of plants to flower or fruit, or that the shape will be spoilt or, in the worst scenario, that the plant will be killed. However, take comfort from the knowledge that you are unlikely to kill a plant by pruning it, as plants are surprisingly resilient. The worst that can happen is that you may lose a season's flowers or fruit,

and even then, you will probably find that the plant will perform better than ever the following year.

More important is the need to grasp a few basic principles and to watch your plants to discover how they grow and flower. Different techniques will yield different results, so adopt the approach that best suits you and your style of gardening.

Some gardeners like the garden to look tidy with everything tightly controlled and clipped to shape. This can be

Above: Shrub roses are usually quite large and bushy but they still benefit from pruning.

Right: Clematis 'Barbara Dibley' needs selective pruning in early spring for a flush of flowers in late spring and summer.

rewarding but is also time-consuming. Others take a more relaxed approach, often through necessity. The overall appearance of their gardens may be less regimented, but the plants will still be healthy and will perform well.

BUILDING CONFIDENCE

The best way to learn to prune is to do it, then to observe the results. You will soon discover which methods produce the effect you want. You can then apply the same technique to other similar plants.

Always remember that pruning is not always strictly necessary. If a plant pleases you exactly the way it is, you can often leave it alone as long as it remains healthy and productive. However, this does not mean that you

should allow your plants to grow unchecked for years, and then attack them with the shears only when they have got out of hand.

Prune a plant indiscriminately at the wrong time and in the wrong way and it may well regrow with redoubled vigour, making it much more of a problem than it was in the first place. If you have any serious doubts, prune lightly; you can always do a little more trimming later if the plant responds well. Alternatively, prune the plant in stages, perhaps a quarter of the growth one year, then, after checking the response, tackling the remainder the following year.

Above: *Pruning climbing roses in spring will encourage stronger growth.*

Left: *A healthy camellia at its peak.*

Introduction

WHY WE NEED TO PRUNE

We prune plants for a variety of reasons: one is to control size and shape. This is especially important in a small garden where space is at a premium. However, the number of plants that you can control in this way is relatively small.

It is better to think of pruning as a means of refreshing the plant, so that it will produce a large proportion of young growth. Young wood flowers and fruits better, provides good, strong material for taking cuttings, and is healthier than the old.

If allowed to build up, old, dead wood can harbour disease. Thinning stems is also a good means of improving air circulation within the body of the plant. If the growth is dense and congested, damp air tends to settle

around the stems, encouraging mildew and other fungal diseases which can only be eliminated with fungicides. These days, gardeners try to keep their use of chemicals in the garden to the absolute minimum, and correct pruning can mean you will not need them.

You can also prune to enhance a particular decorative effect, for example, to give larger leaves, or to encourage a mass of brilliantly coloured young stems. Remember, however, that these techniques usually bring some losses as well as gains. Prune a dogwood hard for its vivid winter stem effect, and you will lose that summer's flowers, because the plant does not have time to grow and ripen sufficiently for flowering. The choice is yours.

Fruit trees and bushes usually have quite specific needs, in order to help them produce the biggest crop. Turn to any pruning manual and you will find a number of complicated procedures, most of which have been developed by professional fruit-growers whose livelihood depends on a large crop. There is no need to worry about those methods as you can easily

Left: Pruning a late-flowering clematis in late winter produces abundant blooms.

achieve yields good enough for the average family using the simplified methods described in this book.

WHEN TO PRUNE

The important thing to remember is that pruning always stimulates new growth, from the point at which you cut. For this reason, it is unwise to prune after midsummer and into autumn. The plant will put on a spurt of fresh, sappy growth that will not have time to harden before the onset of winter, and will probably die back.

NEW WOOD OR OLD?

The first rule in pruning is to make the cut on the correct part of the stem, so it is important to be able to recognize new and old wood. Sometimes also called the current season's growth new wood is supple and bright green in colour, gradually turning brown in summer as it becomes progressively less pliable. One-year-old wood is usually brown. Older wood tends to be grey.

MAKING THE CUTS

Depending on the plant, growth buds either lie opposite each other on the stem or are arranged alternately.

In both cases, you need to cut back to just above a growth bud. In the case of plants with opposite buds, two new shoots will grow, making a bushier

Right: Rambling roses flower once on old wood.

This year's growth – greener and flexible

Last summer's growth – darker and less flexible

Two-year-old wood – darker, thicker and more rigid.

plant. With alternate buds, a new shoot will emerge growing in the direction the bud was pointing. This is why you often hear about cutting back to an outward-facing bud, a method that creates a vase-shaped plant with an open centre through which air can circulate freely.

MAKING A GOOD CUT

1 Cut about 5mm (¼in) above a bud, angled so that moisure runs away from the bud and not into it. If the plant has buds lying opposite one another, cut straight across the stem, just above a strong pair of buds.

2 Avoid leaving a long stump as this will be starved of sap and may rot back.

3 Avoid cutting too close to the bud as this may allow infection to enter.

4 Blunt secateurs (pruning shears) or careless use may bruise or tear the stem instead of cutting through it cleanly. This is an invitation for disease spores to enter. The stump is also too long.

5 If the cut slopes downwards towards the bud, the excessive moisture that may collect in the area could cause the stem to rot.

6 Shrubs with opposite leaves should be treated in a different way to those with leaves that form an alternate leaf arrangement. Cut straight across the stem, just above a strong pair of buds.

HOW TO USE THIS BOOK

The book is arranged so that the basic principles of pruning various well-known and popular plants are explained in detail. Drawings are included for each pruning method showing clearly how the cuts should be made. Read the book through and you will soon discover that many of the techniques are similar – because the principles of pruning remain the same whatever type of plant you are dealing with.

Roses and clematis have specific needs depending on the variety. Use a good rose catalogue if you are unsure which type of rose you have. Clematis are divided into three groups, and·this information is usually stated on the plant label when you buy your plant. If in doubt, the section on clematis will help you ascertain to which group your plant belongs.

The book begins with details of basic pruning equipment that you will need. At the back of the book, a quick reference chart provides appropriate pruning methods for each plant, with the exception of roses, clematis and fruits, which have specific needs. This is followed by charts outlining pruning by season and common plant names.

This books does not deal with tree pruning. If you have a large tree that needs attention, it is best to contact a qualified professional. Ask at your local nursery or garden centre for their recommendations.

Saws & Power Tools

GOOD-QUALITY TOOLS ALWAYS MAKE THE JOB EASIER. SHARP BLADES MAKE CLEAN CUTS THAT HEAL RAPIDLY.

GRECIAN SAW

This is a good general-purpose pruning saw. It has a curved blade that narrows towards the tip, making it easy to use among congested branches. It is also easy to use above head height, because the backward-pointing teeth cut on the pull stroke.

STRAIGHT PRUNING SAW

This is a general-purpose pruning saw for cutting through thicker branches on trees and shrubs. Avoid those with teeth on both sides of the blade: these can accidentally damage branches you wish to retain.

BOW SAW

Because this saw is designed to cut on both the pull and push strokes, it cuts fast and is useful for making horizontal cuts low down on a plant. However, it is difficult to use in a confined space.

POWERED HEDGE TRIMMERS

Electrically powered models are suitable for most gardens. They can be mains or battery powered, but mains-driven types are the best option, as they can be used for longer periods of time. Always carry the cable over your shoulder to avoid accidents. Battery-driven models are useful for a small or remote hedge, where access is difficult with a cable, but the charge may not last long enough for a very long hedge without recharging.

If you have a long stretch of hedge to cut, use a petrol- (gasoline-) driven model, which can usually be hired from tool shops.

SAFETY TIPS

• Electrically powered tools must be used with a circuit breaker.

• Wear goggles to protect your eyes and (if necessary) ear defenders to protect your ears.

• Never use power tools when standing on a stepladder as your balance will be affected.

• Do not use electrical equipment during or just after rain.

Equipment
Small Hand Tools

Although most of us can manage with a good pair of secateurs (pruning shears or pruners), long-handled pruners (loppers or lopping shears) and hand shears, there are times when more specialist tools are required.

Bypass secateurs
(Pruning shears)
Good secateurs (pruning shears) are suitable for a range of pruning jobs. Bypass secateurs have a broad concave or square blade that cuts against a narrower, hooked blade that holds the branch while the cut is made.

*Bypass secateurs
(pruning shears)*

Anvil secateurs
(Pruning shears)
These have a straight blade that cuts against a flat anvil, often with a groove cut in it through which sap can drain away. Ensure that the blade is kept sharp to avoid crushing the stems.

*Anvil secateurs
(pruning shears)*

If you have a weak grip, ratchet shears may be more appropriate. The ratchet device enables you to cut through the stem in several small movements that require less effort.

Most secateurs will cut stems up to 1cm (½in) thick.

Long-handled pruners
(Loppers or lopping shears)
These can be used to cut through stems that are too thick to be cut with secateurs. They are useful for reaching into the base of a plant (particularly if you find bending difficult) or for branches above eye level.

*Long-handled pruners
(loppers or lopping shears)*

10

Pruning knife

Hand shears with a straight blade

Hand shears with a wavy blade

TREE PRUNERS

(Tree loppers or pole pruners)

For tall shrubs, these will make the job easier. Long-handled pruners do not reach as high and can be tiring to use above shoulder level.

The mechanism by which these work varies with the make: they may be operated by rope, metal rods, or fixed or telescopic handles. The small lever mechanism in the handle transfers the cutting action to the cutting head. The hooked end makes it easier to position and steadies the tool while cutting.

PRUNING KNIFE

These knives usually have curved, folding blades that make it easier to ensure the blade cuts into the shoot as you cut towards yourself with a slicing motion.

Because of the temptation to use the thumb as an anvil, such knives must be used with great care.

SHEARS

Mainly used for hedge trimming, shears can also be used for cutting through branches on shrubs and trees that are too thick for secateurs or loppers, provided there is a notch at the base of the blades. They can also be used to trim low-growing shrubs such as heathers and ground-cover roses. Some models have blades with wavy edges that help trap and hold the shoots while cutting.

Make sure you choose shears of a weight you feel comfortable with; cutting a hedge by hand can be tiring work.

11

Coppicing & Pollarding

THESE METHODS, CARRIED OUT IN EARLY SPRING TO DOGWOODS AND
SOME WILLOWS, ARE USED TO ENHANCE THE COLOUR OF ORNAMEN-
TAL STEMS OR THE LEAVES, OR TO RESTRICT TREE SIZE.

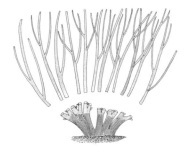

Left: *To coppice, cut back all the recent growth in late winter to early spring, leaving a low woody mound (or 'stool').*

Below: Rubus cockburnianus, *coppiced for winter effect.*

PLANTS TO TRY

Catalpa bignonioides
Cornus sibirica
Cornus stolonifera
Eucalyptus gunnii
Paulownia tomentosa
Rubus cockburnianus
Salix alba vitellina

1 For coppicing, pruning is simple but severe. Cut back stems to near ground level leaving a low, woody framework. Do this early every spring or every other spring if the plant is still young.

2 A coppiced shrub will look like this at the start of the growing season. The technique is a useful means of restricting the size of plants that could otherwise grow too big.

Above: The colourful stems of a pollarded
Salix Alba vitelina *'Britzensis' in full glory*
during the winter months.

1 Allow the plant to grow unpruned until
the trunk has reached the desired height.

2 In late winter or spring, cut the stems
back hard near to the top of the trunk to
leave very short stubs. A mass of new
shoots will be produced over the summer
that will create a colourful winter effect.

PLANTS TO TRY

Catalpa bignonioides
Eucalyptus gunnii
Paulownia tomentosa
Robinia pseudoacacia
Tilia

3 Over time the pollarded head becomes
more stubby and will produce fine colourful stems annually.

4 If possible, feed immediately after
pruning to give the plant a boost and to
achieve the desired growth.

13

Cutting Back to a Framework

SHRUBS THAT FLOWER ON SHOOTS PRODUCED IN THE CURRENT YEAR WILL BECOME INCREASINGLY STRAGGLY UNLESS THEY ARE PRUNED ANNUALLY. PRUNING WILL PROMOTE BLOOMS CLOSER TO THE GROUND.

Left: Prune hard annually to a low frame-work of old, darker wood to encourage a mass of new shoots and a bushy habit.

Below: Buddleja davidii *produces masses of flowers when pruned this way.*

PLANTS TO TRY

Buddleja davidii
Caryopteris
Hydrangea paniculata
Sambucus racemosa

1 In late winter to early spring, before new growth starts, cut back to a low framework no higher than 90cm (3ft).

2 You can also prune harder, cutting the thicker stems flush with the ground. If you delay pruning until early spring, new growth from the base of the plant will be clearly visible.

Cutting to the Ground

THIS TECHNIQUE IS OFTEN USED ON LATE-FLOWERING SHRUBS OF
BORDERLINE HARDINESS THAT TEND TO DIE BACK IN WINTER. LEAVE
THE STEMS OVER WINTER TO PROVIDE FROST PROTECTION.

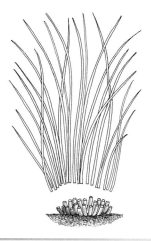

Left: Cut back all the previous year's
growth just above the ground each spring.

Below: Fuchsia 'Tom Thumb' benefits
from a pruned framework after the winter.

PLANTS TO TRY

Ceratostigma willmottianum
Cestrum parqui
Fuchsia (hardy varieties)
Perovskia atriplicifolia

1 In early spring, as soon as new growth is
visible, cut the previous year's stems back
hard, flush with the ground or close to it.

2 After pruning, the plant has more access
to the light and will grow away strongly.
This will create a bushy, compact plant.

Deadheading with Shears

REMOVING FADED FLOWERS IS A FORM OF PRUNING. IN THE CASE OF HEATHERS (*CALLUNA*, *DABOECIA* AND *ERICA*) IT IS EASIEST TO SHEAR THEM OFF IN ONE GO.

Above: *Trim back heathers as the flowers begin to fade, being careful not to cut back into the darker, old wood.*

Above: *Pruning to keep heathers compact will give you a neat heather bed.*

1 Shear over your plants, cutting just below the flower spike. Heathers will not regenerate from cuts made into old, bare wood. If pruning winter-flowering heathers, wait until the spring to ensure you do not damage tender growth.

2 Some heathers are grown for their coloured foliage rather than their flowers, which in a few cases clash. In winter, lightly trim back the developing flowers before they have the chance to open. This will encourage further leaf growth.

16

Clipping

MANY EVERGREENS RESPOND WELL TO BEING CLIPPED TO SHAPE, EITHER WITH SHEARS OR (IF THE LEAVES ARE LARGE) WITH SECATEURS (PRUNERS). WITH PRACTICE YOU CAN CREATE UNUSUAL TOPIARY.

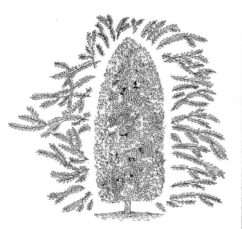

Above: *Trim new growth to shape in spring and midsummer.*

Above: *Yew is the classic shrub to clip into a toparian shape.*

1 Trim off as much as necessary of the new growth, but avoid cutting back into old wood. Shear the plants twice during the growing season to produce a smooth surface. Practise topiary on quick-growing plants such as *Ligustrum vulgare* before progressing to more ambitious schemes.

PLANTS TO TRY

Berberis
Buxus sempervirens
Ligustrum vulgare
Lonicera nitida
Osmanthus decorus
Phillyrea angustifolia
Prunus lusitanica
Taxus baccata

17

Large-leaved Evergreens

MOST EVERGREEN SHRUBS GROW HAPPILY WITHOUT ROUTINE PRUN-
ING, BUT IF YOU HAVE A SMALL GARDEN YOU MAY WANT TO RESTRICT
THE SIZE OF LARGER SHRUBS.

Above: Prune out awkwardly placed stems
and some of the older growth. You can
also shorten stems that have flowered,
cutting back just above a growth bud.

Above: Most larger leaved evergreens only
need pruning when they need restricting.

If a shrub produces a wayward shoot that
spoils the outline of the plant, cut it back to
its point of origin, reaching right into the
plant if necessary. This will restore its uni-
form shape.

Variegated evergreens, such as this holly,
sometimes produce plain green shoots.
These are always more vigorous than the
typical growth and should be cut out
entirely as soon as you spot them.

The 'One-third' Method

THIS SIMPLE TECHNIQUE WORKS ON A WIDE VARIETY OF ORNAMENTAL FLOWERING SHRUBS. IT IS A GOOD WAY TO KEEP THEM COMPACT AND FRESH, AND IT ENCOURAGES HEALTHY BLOOMS.

Above: Cut out one-third of the oldest stems close to ground level.

PLANTS TO TRY

Cornus (grown for foliage effect,
e.g. *C. alba* 'Elegantissima'
and 'Spaethii')
Cotinus coggygria
Forsythia
Hypericum
Kerria japonica 'Pleniflora'
Kolkwitzia
Leycesteria
Philadelphus
Potentilla (shrubby types)
Ribes sanguineum
Spiraea

1 Immediately after flowering, cut back a third of the oldest stems, cutting some back to strong buds low down and removing others at or near ground level. At the same time, remove any weak or badly placed branches and shorten any damaged stems. This technique is satisfactory for established plants only, and is unsuitable for any under three years old.

Above: Kolkwitzia amabilis *pruned by one-third will keep the shrub compact.*

19

Shortening New Growth

A LIGHT TRIMMING WILL ENCOURAGE A BUSHIER HABIT ON PLANTS
SUCH AS *CYSTISUS* AND *GENISTA* THAT OTHERWISE CAN EASILY
BECOME GAUNT WITH LONG, BARE BRANCHES.

GARDENER'S TIP
Use this method on young plants only. Old, neglected plants will not respond well and are best replaced.

Below: *This* Genista lydia *is covered with flowers the year following pruning.*

Above: *Trim back the new growth by half after flowering. Be careful not to cut back into older wood.*

1 Immediately after flowering, shorten the previous season's growth, which will be pale and supple, by about half. Take care not to cut back into old wood.

2 A light trimming is all that will be necessary on some of the stems. Ensure that you cut recent growth only of that made last summer.

Shortening Side Shoots

SHRUBS THAT FLOWER ON THE PREVIOUS YEAR'S SHOOTS OFTEN BENE-
FIT FROM A LIGHT PRUNING AFTER FLOWERING. THIS WILL ENCOUR-
AGE MORE BLOOMS THE FOLLOWING YEAR.

Above: *Trim back shoots that have flowered
(shown here in yellow) by between a half
and two-thirds of their length.*

PLANTS TO TRY
Cistus
Convolvulus cneorum
Helianthemum
Kalmia latifolia

Below: *A* cistus *in full flower.*

1 Immediately after flowering, trim back
only the shoots that have flowered. Shorten
the current season's growth, which will still
be soft and pliable, by up to two-thirds.
Make sure you do not cut into older,
darker wood.

Plants in this category keep a good shape
whether you prune or not, but a light trimming results in more side shoots which will
all be flower-bearers the following year.

21

Grey-leaved Foliage Plants

MANY GREY-LEAVED PLANTS LOOK UNATTRACTIVE IF ALLOWED TO
BECOME STRAGGLY. ANNUAL PRUNING WILL KEEP THEM LOOKING
FRESH AND WELL-CLOTHED WITH FOLIAGE.

> ### PLANTS TO TRY
>
> *Artemisia* (shrubby types)
> *Helichrysum italicum*
> *Lavandula*
> *Santolina chamaecyparissus*

*Above: Cut back grey-leaved plants to as
low down on the stem as possible, just
above a new growth bud.*

Above: A Santolina chamaecyparissus *that
has become leggy.*

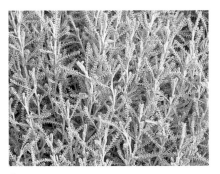

1 In early spring, as the new growth
emerges, prune back the previous year's
growth, cutting just above a new shoot or
a developing bud. The plant will look
sparse when you have finished.

2 The plant will soon be well-clothed with
new leaves. You need to start this regime
early in the life of the plant: most grey-
leaved plants will not regenerate well if you
cut into very old wood.

Rejuvenating the Neglected

OLD AND NEGLECTED SHRUBS OFTEN NEED TO BE REPLACED, BUT IT IS WORTH TRYING SOME DRASTIC PRUNING FIRST. IF THE SHRUB DOESN'T RESPOND, THEN REPLACE IT.

Above: Staggering drastic pruning is often effective. Here, the central stem has been left unpruned. Two stems pruned hard last year have produced fresh growth, so it is safe to cut back the two old branches as shown to encourage further growth.

Above: New shoots will soon appear.

1 In late winter to early spring, cut back all the stems to just above ground level. If you would prefer to be more cautious, cut the shrub back in stages as shown in the illustration. Prune back one-third of the stems in the first year, a second third in the next. Cut back the remainder the following year.

2 Trim any ragged edges with a pruning knife or rasp to prevent infection entering the wound. If the shrub shows no sign of life in the first year after pruning, dig it up and replace it.

23

Floribunda Roses

SOMETIMES CALLED CLUSTER-FLOWERED ROSES, FLORIBUNDAS ARE NOTED FOR THEIR PROLIFIC BLOOMING.

Above: Cut out damaged, badly placed, and weak shoots, then shorten the remainder by between a half and two-thirds of their length.

Above: Rosa 'Sexy Rexy'.

1 In early spring, cut back all dead, diseased and damaged stems, cutting them back to their point of origin, if necessary.

2 Remove any crossing or awkwardly placed shoots that are growing into the centre of the bush.

3 Shorten the remaining stems by up to two-thirds of their length, cutting back to healthy buds that are pointing outwards. Prune vigorous varieties lightly, weaker-growing plants harder.

4 During the flowering season, remove spent flower trusses to encourage the plant to flower further.

Hybrid Tea Roses

ALSO KNOWN AS LARGE-FLOWERED ROSES, HYBRID TEAS HAVE LARGE, FULLY DOUBLE FLOWERS WITH A HIGH-CENTRE. THEIR BEAUTIFUL BLOOMS ARE PERFECT FOR FLORAL DISPLAYS.

Above: Cut out badly placed, diseased or dead wood to the base. Shorten all other stems by about half.

Above: Rosa 'Savoy Hotel'.

1 In early spring, cut out any diseased or dead shoots, as well as any stems that are badly placed or rub against each other. Most of these can be cut back to their point of origin, but if growth is sparse, cut to just above a healthy bud.

2 Prune the remaining stems by about half, or to within 20–25cm (8–10in) of the ground. Always cut to an outward-facing bud.

3 During the flowering season, remove spent flowers to prolong the display.

Shrub Roses

WILD ROSES AND OLD-FASHIONED VARIETIES OF ROSES THAT PRE-DATE HYBRID TEAS AND FLORIBUNDAS ARE KNOWN AS SHRUB ROSES. THEY GENERALLY FLOWER FOR A FAIRLY SHORT PERIOD.

Above: *Shorten main stems by about a quarter to a half, side shoots by up to two-thirds. Cut out weak and badly placed stems entirely.*

Above: Rosa 'Frühlingsgold'.

1 Pruning prevents shrub roses becoming congested, improves their appearance and increases the number of blooms. In early spring, thin any congested growth by cutting back older stems at ground level.

2 Shorten main shoots by up to a half. Some need only light trimming.

3 Side shoots can be shortened by up to two-thirds to balance the framework.

Standard Roses

PRUNE STANDARD ROSES IN EARLY SPRING TO FORM AN ATTRACTIVE, ROUNDED HEAD. WEEPING STANDARDS ARE PRUNED IN SUMMER TO RETAIN THEIR FLOWING APPEARANCE.

Above: Shorten the previous season's growth by about a half (left). On a weeping standard, cut back the trailing shoots to new buds in the crown when flowering has finished (right).

Above: Standard roses need staking to keep them upright.

1 In early spring, shorten the previous year's main stems on standard roses to about six buds from the base, cutting to outward-facing buds. Aim to create a balanced shape, but do not prune too hard or new over-vigorous shoots may spoil the shape.

2 Shorten side shoots to a couple of buds. To stop the growth becoming congested cut back dead or diseased wood.

3 Remove the flowers as they fade to prolong the display.

Climbing Roses

PROLIFIC CLIMBING ROSES ARE USUALLY REPEAT-FLOWERING, OFTEN ON A COMBINATION OF THE OLD AND NEW WOOD. THEY ARE FREQUENTLY HIGHLY SCENTED AS WELL AS IMPRESSIVE TO LOOK AT.

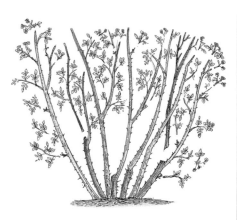

Above: Cut some of the oldest stems back to strong new shoots near the base or where there is a suitable replacement. Shorten laterals by up to two-thirds.

Above: The magnificent wall-mounted Rosa 'Climbing Iceberg'.

1 In the first few years after planting, the aim is to build up a framework of branches on the chosen support. In spring, cut back any older, unproductive shoots, but do not remove more than one-third of the stems or flowering will suffer next year.

2 In summer, tie in vigorous shoots as they grow, using soft string. Do not tie too tightly – you may chafe the stems.

3 Cut back the faded flowers to encourage further flowering.

Rambling Roses

THESE ROSES FLOWER ONCE, ON THE OLD WOOD. THEY THEN PRO-
DUCE A MASS OF NEW GROWTH NEAR TO THE BASE.

*Above: Remove very old or diseased stems
entirely. Cut back old canes that have
flowered to a point where there is
vigorous replacement growth.*

Above: Ramblers, such as Rosa 'Rambling
Rector', *should be pruned after flowering.*

1 In late summer, after flowering, cut out
all dead or damaged shoots, as well as any
that are weak and spindly.

2 Shorten older canes that have flowered
to vigorous new shoots. You will probably
be able to leave a proportion unpruned.

3 Tie in the new shoots to the support. Try
to pull them to the horizontal – they will
produce more flower-bearing laterals for
next year.

4 On the canes that remain, shorten the
side shoots to two or three leaves.

Clematis

THESE POPULAR CLIMBERS ARE DIVIDED INTO THREE GROUPS, EACH
FLOWERING AT DIFFERENT TIMES OF THE YEAR. THE GROUPS ALSO
HAVE DIFFERENT PRUNING REQUIREMENTS.

Elegant clematis climb by means of curling leaf stalks, and are attractive against walls or on fences (fitted with trellis supports), over pergolas, or growing through other plants. Vigorous species also look spectacular when grown through trees.

For pruning purposes, clematis are usually divided into three groups, depending on when they flower. These groups are recognized within the nursery business, and most clematis on sale will state on the label to which group they belong.

Group 1 clematis flower from late winter to spring on wood made the previous year, and often have small flowers. Several species fall into this group.

Group 2 consists of large-flowered hybrids that flower in late spring and early summer, on wood made the previous year, then again in mid- to late summer on the new wood. The group includes some species with double flowers. However, the flowers in the second flush are always single.

Group 3 clematis flower from midsummer to autumn on the current season's growth. The group includes many large-flowered hybrids, as well as texensis types with flowers like miniature tulips and viticella types with flowers that open flat. There are also several notable species: the yellow-flowered *C. tibetana* subsp. *vernayi*, and *C. flammula* and *C. rehderiana*.

Above: C. 'Fireworks' is one of the most spectacular clematis with large luminous violet flowers.

GARDENER'S TIP

Training is vital and should begin early. Tie the stems to the horizontal as far as is possible as they grow, but take great care: the stems are brittle and are easily broken.

Group 1 Clematis

THIS GROUP COMPRISES THOSE CLEMATIS THAT FLOWER BEFORE MID-SUMMER, ON SHOOTS PRODUCED THE PREVIOUS YEAR. PRUNE ONLY TO KEEP THE PLANT WITHIN BOUNDS.

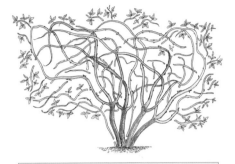

Left: Shorten only those stems that have outgrown their allotted space and cut out a proportion of the remainder to relieve congestion. Otherwise, this group can be left unpruned.

GARDENER'S TIP

If a group 1 clematis has been allowed to get out of control, has tangled stems and is bare at the base, you can renovate it by cutting it all back to near ground level. Regeneration can be slow, however, and it might be a couple of years before the plant is flowering freely again.

Above: C. montana *var.* rubens 'Continuity' requires only light pruning.

1 Immediately after flowering, cut back to their point of origin any stems that have outgrown their allotted space. Do this only when absolutely necessary, however.

2 Thin congested growth if necessary. After pruning, the plant will look neater at the edges but overall few shoots will have been removed.

31

Group 2 Clematis

THESE CLEMATIS FLOWER TWICE: IN LATE SPRING OR EARLY SUMMER ON WOOD MADE THE PREVIOUS YEAR, AND IN MID- TO LATE SUMMER ON THE CURRENT SEASON'S GROWTH.

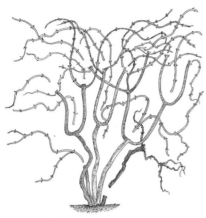

Above: *Prune selectively in early spring. Cut out old, damaged and weak shoots, thin tangled growth, but leave a good proportion unpruned.*

GARDENER'S TIP

You can also prune group 2 clematis as for group 3. You will lose the first crop of flowers, but the second will be more spectacular. Double-flowered types will only produce single flowers, however.

1 Cut back any dead or damaged stems to near ground level. Shorten any stems that have outgrown their allotted space.

2 Leave some of the growth unpruned, and respace shoots to fill the gaps. These will carry the first crop of flowers.

Above: *Group 2 Clematis 'Royalty' produces glorious double purple flowers twice each year.*

Group 3 Clematis

THESE CLEMATIS FLOWER FROM MIDSUMMER TO AUTUMN. THE GROUP INCLUDES SEVERAL SPECIES, MANY LARGE-FLOWERED HYBRIDS AND THE TEXENSIS AND VITICELLA TYPES.

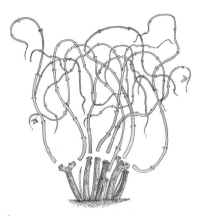

Left: Pruning a group 3 clematis is basically a matter of renovation. In late winter, cut back all the previous year's growth to the lowest set of strong buds on each stem to leave a woody framework.

> ### GARDENER'S TIP
> For a late crop of flowers, delay pruning until mid-spring.

1 In late winter, cut back all the growth to a pair of strong buds low down on the stem. Any obviously dead stems can be cut off at ground level.

2 If you want the flowers high up the plant, for example to cover the top of a pergola, cut back higher on the stem. This method particularly suits vigorous species and the stunning yellow-flowered C 'Bill MacKenzie'.

Above: The enduringly popular C. 'Jackmanii Superba'.

Honeysuckle

LONICERA (HONEYSUCKLES) NEED LITTLE PRUNING WHEN YOUNG, BUT WITH AGE CAN EASILY DEVELOP A TANGLE OF UNPRODUCTIVE STEMS THAT FLOWER ONLY ABOVE EYE LEVEL.

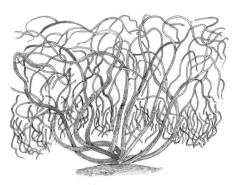

Above: *Shortening congested stems will control the spread of a honeysuckle.*

Right: *Regular pruning of Honeysuckles will ensure an even distribution of flowers.*

1 In late winter to early spring, when the stems are bare and you can see what you are doing, shear back dead and congested stems, cutting just above strong buds. You can be fairly brutal. Honeysuckles are vigorous plants that seem to thrive on rough treatment.

2 If the plant is hopelessly tangled, cut back all stems to a height of 30–60cm (1–2ft) from the ground, using loppers if necessary. Flowering in the next season will not be prolific, but the plant will soon return to its full glory. You can train the new shoots to a support as they appear.

Wisteria

THIS IS A VIGOROUS PLANT THAT PRODUCES A VAST QUANTITY OF LEAFY STEMS ANNUALLY. CAREFUL PRUNING DIVERTS ITS ENERGIES INTO FLOWER PRODUCTION.

Above: After flowering, wisterias suddenly produce a mass of new stems. Cut back any that are not needed to extend the framework. Shorten this growth further in winter.

Above: A wisteria in full flower.

1 Throughout the growing season, train in the new stems that are needed to extend the framework. Once this is established, in late summer shorten the new growth to between four and six leaves to restrict the spread of the plant.

2 In late winter, shorten the pruned stems still further to two or three buds. This typically means leaving the summer's growth reduced to just 7.5–10cm (3–4in). Over time the plant develops a system of spurs that carry the flowers.

Other Climbers

CLIMBERS ARE NATURALLY VIGOROUS PLANTS THAT CAN EASILY BECOME CONGESTED. PRUNING IS EASIEST TO DO WHEN THE STEMS ARE BARE IN WINTER AND YOU CAN SEE WHAT YOU ARE DOING.

Above: *When pruning climbers, cut out older, unproductive stems to the base and shorten other stems as necessary.*

Right: Solanum crispum *'Glasnevin'*.

1 In winter cut out old, dead wood completely. You may need to shorten long stems bit by bit if they are very congested. Shorten any overlong but otherwise healthy and supple stems.

2 Tie in the remaining shoots to create a balanced framework of stems. Although the plant will probably occupy a similar area, the growth should look less congested and more evenly balanced.

Wall-trained Chaenomeles

SOMETIMES KNOWN AS ORNAMENTAL QUINCES OR JAPONICA, *CHAENOMELES* ARE VALUED FOR THEIR ATTRACTIVE FLOWERS IN LATE WINTER. WALL-TRAINED SPECIMENS NEED ANNUAL TRIMMING.

Above: Chaenomeles *should be trained espalier-fashion as shown. Once the espalier is established, shortening the side shoots in summer will help display the flowers.*

Above: The bright, waxy flowers of Chaenomeles speciosa *'Cardinalis'.*

1 As they grow, tie in strong shoots to the horizontal to extend the framework. This will help maintain a neat and controlled shape.

2 In summer, shorten sideshoots growing away from the main stem to five leaves. Remove entirely any that are growing towards the wall or are awkwardly placed.

Wall-trained Pyracanthas

PYRACANTHAS ARE POPULAR AS WALL-SHRUBS, EITHER TRAINED AS ESPALIERS OR MORE INFORMALLY TIED BACK, DEPENDING ON THE EFFECT YOU WISH TO CREATE.

Above: On wall-trained pyracanthas, shorten side shoots in midsummer to expose the berries.

Right: Pyracanthas are grown mainly for their brilliantly coloured berries.

1 Tie in new shoots tight to the wall to create an espalier or fan shape. Alternatively, simply pin back the strongest shoots and allow the others to billow forward.

2 In midsummer, remove any wayward or awkwardly placed shoots as these will induce spur-like shoots. Shorten other side shoots to expose the ripening berries.

Ornamental Vines

VINES, SUCH AS *VITIS COIGNETIAE* AND *V. VINIFERA* 'PURPUREA', ARE OFTEN GROWN OVER A FRAMEWORK. UNLESS YOU ADOPT A METHODICAL APPROACH TO PRUNING, THEY WILL BECOME TANGLED.

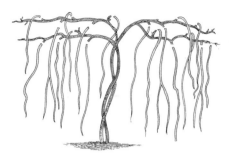

Above: A vine that has been trained over a pergola or similar support will produce stems that cascade downwards. Prune these back close to the main stem when the plant is dormant.

Right: A well-pruned ornamental vine provides neat and even coverage.

1 Train the stems horizontally over the support until you have achieved the desired coverage. Once established, each winter cut back the previous season's growth to within one or two buds of its point of origin, to keep the plant tidy.

2 Over the years, short spurs (stubs) will form along the main framework of branches. Cut new growth back to these each winter to produce a fresh curtain of new shoots each summer without the tangled growth that would otherwise develop.

39

Conifers

GENERALLY, CONIFERS ARE TROUBLE-FREE PLANTS THAT THRIVE WITHOUT REGULAR PRUNING. HOWEVER, YOU MAY OCCASIONALLY EXPERIENCE THE PROBLEMS DESCRIBED HERE.

Above: Conifers with a spreading habit may grow so wide that they begin to encroach on a path or surrounding plants. Cut back offending branches to a point where the cuts are hidden by other branches that cover them.

Right: A group of dwarf conifers.

REMOVING A COMPETING LEADER

1 To ensure a straight, single stem, where two or more leaders have formed, leave the strongest unpruned. Cut the other back to its point of origin to prevent further competition and loss of vigour.

2 If the remaining leader is not growing strongly upright, tie a cane to the conifer's main stem. Tie the new leader to the cane to encourage vertical growth. Once this is established, the cane can be removed.

CUTTING BACK UNCHARACTERISTIC GROWTH

Conifers have two different types of foliage: juvenile and adult. Sometimes a conifer retains its juvenile form but may produce adult shoots. If the conifer throws out a stem that is uncharacteristic, it will spoil the overall appearance of the plant, if allowed to remain. Cut back the stem to its point of origin, reaching into the heart of the plant if necessary.

Below: This Cedrus atlantica 'Glauca Pendula' has a naturally arching habit. Removing the leader has encouraged it to spread far and wide. The horizontal branches will need support as they age.

SHAPING CONIFERS

Though most conifers achieve a pleasing profile of their own accord, you can also clip them, provided you do this regularly and do not cut back into old wood. In spring or summer, lightly trim the conifer with shears or secateurs (pruners).

REMOVING DEAD PATCHES

Dead patches occasionally appear on conifers, sometimes as the result of drought or very cold winds. Prune out the dead growth, cutting back to live wood. If this results in an unsightly gap in the coverage, loosely tie in some of the surrounding stems to cover the gap.

New Hedges

IF THEY ARE TO PROVIDE A THICK, EVEN BARRIER, HEDGES NEED PRUNING FROM THE VERY START. CUT THEM BACK WHEN YOU PLANT THEM TO ENSURE THEY BRANCH NEAR TO THE BASE.

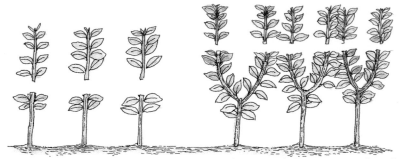

Above: *Shorten the stems on newly planted hedges by up to a half to encourage branching close to the base (left). Once the new growth appears, shorten this as well, to make bushier plants (right).*

GARDENER'S TIP

When buying hedging material, young plants make sense. They are not only very cheap, but also establish much more quickly than the more expensive larger ones.

---

1 Hedges are best planted in spring or autumn. They are usually purchased as young plants with a single straight stem. To ensure they bush out properly, cut them back by up to one half of their length when you plant them.

2 The following summer, trim the new shoots back by about a half to encourage further branching from near to the base of the plant. This will encourage a thick, bushy habit.

Above: *Box is an excellent hedging plant.*

Formal Hedges

CLASSIC FORMAL HEDGES GIVE STYLE AND ELEGANCE TO A GARDEN. THE SIMPLE TECHNIQUES DESCRIBED HERE WILL KEEP THEM LOOKING WELL SHAPED AND SMART.

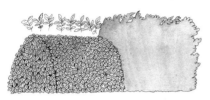

Above: Cut the sides so that they slope towards the top. A flat top is easier to clip than a curved one (top). A rounded top is attractive, but you need a good eye to keep it even (bottom).

PLANTS TO TRY
Buxus sempervirens
Buxus sempervirens 'suffruticosa'
x *Cupressocyparis leylandii*
Taxus baccata

Above: A carefully clipped yew.

1 Clip established formal hedges twice a year, in mid-spring and midsummer. To make sure you cut the top straight, run a string between two uprights and check the level with a spirit level. Hold the shears flat and horizontal when trimming the top.

2 Shear over the surface of the hedge, holding the blades flat against the surface. Using power tools (see inset) can speed up the job considerably. Use an even, wide, sweeping motion, keeping the blade parallel to the hedge.

43

Informal Flowering Hedges

FLOWERING HEDGES NEED PRUNING AT THE RIGHT TIME IF THE FLOW-ERS ARE NOT TO BE LOST. A CRISP OUTLINE IS NOT EXPECTED, SO PRUNING IS AIMED MAINLY AT RESTRICTING SIZE.

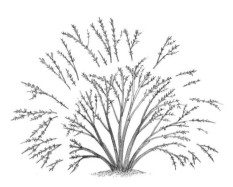

Above: *Restrict pruning to shortening the shoots that have grown since the last prune to maintain a reasonably compact habit. Prune early-flowering hedges immediately after flowering and late-flowering hedges in early spring.*

Above: *Fuchsia makes a delightful informal hedge when it flowers in late summer.*

A hedge of rugosa roses will not need extensive pruning like those used in rose beds, but it is worth cutting damaged, old, tired and woody shoots back to ground level periodically. This will avoid congested growth occuring.

An early-flowering hedge, such as this spiky berberis, can be lightly trimmed immediately after flowering. Simply shear back the flowered growth. The aim is to keep the plants compact and dense rather than to create a formal outline.

Rejuvenating a Neglected Hedge

IT IS SOMETIMES WORTH SALVAGING A NEGLECTED HEDGE THAT
WOULD TAKE YEARS TO REPLACE, BUT CONIFER HEDGES (APART FROM
YEW) WILL NOT RESPOND WELL TO THIS TECHNIQUE.

Above: Cut back all the growth on one side of the hedge to near the base of the shoots. Leave the other side uncut (left). The following year, once new growth has appeared on the cut stems, cut back the other side (right).

Above: A neglected hedge after pruning.

1 This hedge has been neglected and is a mass of tangled shoots. In winter, cut back the top of the hedge by up to 1m (3ft) below the desired height.

> ### GARDENER'S TIP
> If individual plants within the hedge do not regenerate well, dig them up and replace with young specimens.

2 Trim back all the shoots to one side of the hedge, using loppers or a pruning saw, if necessary.

3 Lightly trim new growth that arises from the cut stems once it has reached about 15cm (6in) in length to encourage bushiness. Tackle the other side of the hedge the following year.

45

Dwarf Bush Apple

FOR A SMALL GARDEN, A DWARF BUSH IS USUALLY THE MOST POPULAR OPTION. THIS GIVES YOU A TREE WITH BRANCHES CLOSE TO GROUND LEVEL, MAKING IT EASY TO HARVEST AND PRUNE.

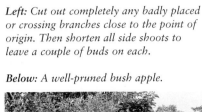

Left: Cut out completely any badly placed or crossing branches close to the point of origin. Then shorten all side shoots to leave a couple of buds on each.

Below: *A well-pruned bush apple.*

GARDENER'S TIP

It is best to buy a tree ready trained that has been grafted onto a dwarfing rootstock.

1 Young trees may not need pruning. Only prune if they begin to look congested or bear less fruit. In winter, when the tree is dormant, remove any congested or crossing branches to keep the centre of the bush open.

2 Cut the previous year's growth by two-thirds to three-quarters. On mature specimens, you can cut some back harder to within one or two buds. Shorten any side shoots on the pruned branches to leave just a couple of buds (see inset).

46

Espalier Apple

COMPACT ESPALIER APPLES ARE PRACTICAL IN CONFINED SPACES AND CAN BE TRAINED ON HORIZONTAL WIRES AGAINST WALLS OR FENCES. THEY CAN BE BOUGHT READY TRAINED.

Above: Espalier apples need pruning towards the end of the growing season to control their shape. Cut back side shoots from the main stems to about three leaves above the basal cluster. Side shoots growing from shoots pruned the previous year can be cut back to just one leaf.

Above: A productive espalier apple.

1 Once the main stem has reached the desired height, cut it back to a bud just above the top wire. Growth is then directed into the horizontal branches.

2 In summer, cut back shoots from the main branches that are more than 23cm (9in) to three leaves above the basal cluster.

3 In winter, when the tree is dormant, cut back any shoots that have grown since the summer prune to about 5cm (2in), to develop a system of short spurs (see inset). Shorten all other long shoots to buds close to the main stem, cutting back to one or two buds. These will bear the next year's crop of fruit.

47

Cordon Apple

ANGLED CORDONS ALLOW YOU TO GROW A NUMBER OF DIFFERENT VARIETIES IN A LIMITED SPACE, BUT REGULAR PRUNING IS ESSENTIAL TO STOP THEM OVERLAPPING EACH OTHER.

GARDENER'S TIP
Prune cordon pears in the same way as apples.

Above: Prune cordons in summer by cutting the current season's growth back to two or three leaves above the basal cluster of leaves (and side shoots on these back to one leaf).

Right: Cordons are economic with space.

1 Between late spring and midsummer, prune back the main stem if it has outgrown its allotted space, to within 1–2.5cm ($\frac{1}{2}$–1in) of the old wood. Repeat annually with any new leaders that form to prevent leggy growth.

2 In mid- to late summer, shorten side shoots from the main stem that are over 23cm (9in) long, so that only three leaves remain above the basal cluster. Cordons can also be pruned in winter in the same way as espaliers.

Raspberries

PRUNING RASPBERRIES DEPENDS ON WHETHER THEY FRUIT ON SHOOTS PRODUCED THE PREVIOUS YEAR (SUMMER-FRUITING) OR IN THE CURRENT YEAR (AUTUMN-FRUITING).

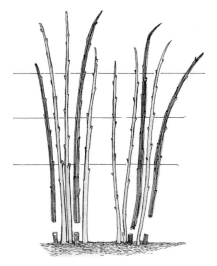

PLANTS TO TRY

Summer fruiting raspberries:
'Glen Coe'
'Glen Moy'
'Leo'
'Malling Admiral'
'Malling Delight'
'Malling Jewel'
'Malling Promise'
Autumn-fruiting raspberries:
'Autumn Bliss'
'Heritage'
'September'
'Zeva Herbsternte'

Above: On summer-fruiters, cut out the shoots that fruited the previous summer and tie in the new canes to replace them.

SUMMER-FRUITING VARIETIES

1 In spring, prune back the old canes, which are darker than the new ones, cutting right back to the base.

2 Tie the new canes to the support. If the clump is very congested, thin the new canes to 7.5cm (3in) apart.

AUTUMN-FRUITING VARIETIES

When dormant in winter, simply cut all the stems back to just above soil level.

Right: The autumn-fruiting 'Zeva Herbsternte'.

Gooseberries

THESE FRUITING PLANTS ARE USUALLY GROWN ON A SHORT LEG OR AS BUSHES. THE MAIN PRUNING IS IN WINTER, BUT YOU CAN THIN THE GROWTH IN SUMMER TO KEEP THE BUSHES OPEN.

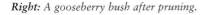

Above: *Shorten the summer's growth at the ends of the main stems by between one-third and a half, then shorten side shoots growing from the main stems to two buds.*

Right: *A gooseberry bush after pruning.*

1 Gooseberries are thorny plants. Wearing gloves, reduce the previous season's growth at the end of each main shoot by between one-third and a half. You should also cut out any low, weak, badly placed or crossing branches.

2 Shorten side shoots arising from the main stems, cutting them back to two buds from the old wood. This will make the plant less congested. After fruiting, you can also thin the new growth to improve air circulation and prevent mildew.

Black, Red & White Currants

PROLIFIC BLACKCURRANTS FRUIT BEST ON YEAR-OLD BRANCHES. RED AND WHITE CURRANTS FRUIT ON SHOOTS THAT ARE AT LEAST TWO YEARS OLD. ALL ARE PRUNED IN WINTER.

Below: White currants ready for picking.

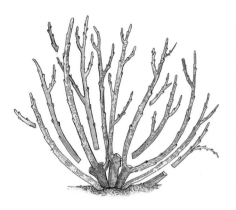

Above: On blackcurrants, cut out some of the oldest wood each year, close to the base where there is a younger shoot to replace it. Also prune any damaged or badly placed branches.

2 For red and white currants, remove one old stem only, pruning just above a bud near ground level.

1 For blackcurrants, remove badly placed branches that are too low or growing inwards. Cut back some of the oldest branches (usually the thickest and darkest) close to the base. Aim to remove one-third.

3 Shorten the wood produced the previous summer by half its length. You can also trim back overlong branches, cutting back to a replacement side shoot.

51

Blackberries & Hybrid Berries

THESE BERRIES (INCLUDING TAYBERRIES AND LOGANBERRIES) ARE EASY TO PRUNE, SINCE MOST FRUIT ON YEAR-OLD CANES.

Left: In winter or early spring, cut back the older shoots that have previously fruited. Tie in the greener shoots made the previous summer.

Below: Ripening blackberries.

PLANTS TO TRY

Blackberries:
'Bedford Giant'
'Himalaya Giant'
'John Innes'
'Smoothstem'
'No Thorn'

Hybrid berries:
Boysenberry
Loganberry
Sunberry
Tayberry
Veitchberry

---

1 Prune out the darker, fruited canes, which grew the previous year, cutting them as close to the ground as possible.

2 Untie the one-year-old canes that have yet to fruit and reposition them in an evenly spaced fan shape. Tie in new shoots as they grow.

Blueberries

THESE ARE SLOW-GROWING PLANTS THAT FRUIT ON BRANCHES TWO TO THREE YEARS OLD. START PRUNING THEM LIGHTLY WHEN THEY ARE THREE OR FOUR YEARS OLD.

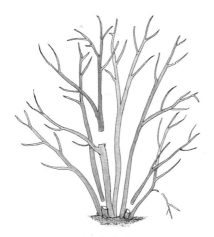

Above: On established plants, prune out older, unproductive wood in spring, cutting back to a vigorous side shoot.

Above: Blueberries when ripe have a whitish bloom which is safe to eat. It is better not to wash berries before eating them.

1 Cut back any unproductive shoots, either to a strong replacement shoot or back to the ground. Do not remove more than one-quarter of the branches.

2 Remove any weak, spindly growth.

PLANTS TO TRY

'Berkeley'
'Bluecrop'
'Bluetta'
'Coville'
'Darrow'
'Earliblue'
'Goldtraube'
'Herbert'
'Ivanhoe'
'Jersey'
'Patriot'

53

Methods of Pruning Chart

NAME OF PLANT	TYPE OF PRUNING	TIME TO PRUNE
Abeliophyllum	No routine pruning	
Abutilon	Shorten side shoots	Summer
Actinidia	As for ornamental vines	Winter
Akebia	No routine pruning	
Artemisia	Cut back hard, if necessary	Early spring
Aucuba	Clip to shape	Spring or summer
Berberis	One-third method	Winter (deciduous); spring (evergreen)
Brachyglottis	Prune to a framework	Early spring
Buddleja	Prune to a framework	Early spring
Buxus	Clip to shape	Spring and summer
Callicarpa	No routine pruning	
Calluna	Deadhead with shears	After flowering
Camellia	No routine pruning	
Campsis	No routine pruning	
Carpenteria	One-third method	Early spring
Caryopteris	Prune to a framework	Early spring
Catalpa bignioides	Coppicing	Early spring
Ceanothus, deciduous	Trim previous year's shoots	Spring

Above: *An elegantly clipped* Buxus.

NAME OF PLANT	TYPE OF PRUNING	TIME TO PRUNE
Ceanothus, evergreen	Shorten side shoots	After flowering
Ceratostigma	Prune to a framework	Early spring
Cestrum parqui	Prune to the base	Early spring
Chaenomeles, wall-trained	Trim previous year's shoots	After flowering
Chimonanthus	One-third method	Spring
Choisya	No routine pruning	
Cistus	Shorten side shoots	After flowering
Clematis	See clematis section	
Clerodendrum	No routine pruning	
Clethra	No routine pruning	
Colutea	One-third method	Early spring
Convolvulus	Shorten side shoots	Late summer
Cornus alba (most cvs)	One-third method	Mid-spring
C. alba 'Sibirica'	Prune hard	Early spring
C. controversa, C. florida	No routine pruning	
C kousa	No routine pruning	
C. stolonifera 'Flaviramea'	Prune hard	Early spring
Corylopsis	No routine pruning	
Corylus	One-third method	Spring
Cotinus	One-third method	Spring
Cotoneaster	One-third method	Winter (deciduous); spring (evergreen)
Cytisus	Shorten new growth	After flowering
Daboecia	Deadhead with shears	After flowering

Above: Clematis montana *needs little pruning.*

Methods of Pruning Chart

NAME OF PLANT	TYPE OF PRUNING	TIME TO PRUNE
Daphne	No routine pruning	
Deutzia	One-third method	After flowering
Elaeagnus	No routine pruning	
Enkianthus	No routine pruning	
Erica	Deadhead with shears	After flowering
Escallonia	One-third method	Late spring
Eucalyptus	Prune to a framework	Early spring
Euonymus	No routine pruning	
Fallopia	One-third method	Spring
Fatsia	No routine pruning	
Forsythia	One-third method	After flowering
Fothergilla	No routine pruning	
Fremontodendron	Shorten side shoots	Spring
Fruits	See individual sections	
Fuchsia, hardy	Prune to the base	Early spring
Garrya	One-third method	Spring
Gaultheria	One-third method	Spring
Genista	Shorten new growth	Late summer
Griselinia	No routine pruning	
x *Halimiocistus*	Shorten side shoots	Late summer
Hebe	No routine pruning	
Hedera	Clip to shape	Summer
Helianthemum	Shorten new shoots	After flowering
Helichrysum	Cut back close to old wood	Early spring

Above: Escallonia *pruned lightly for an informal flowering effect.*

NAME OF PLANT	TYPE OF PRUNING	TIME TO PRUNE
Hibiscus	Prune out old wood	Early spring
Hippophae	One-third method	Spring
Hydrangea macrophylla	Cut back thin shoots; shorten flowered stems	Spring
H. paniculata	Prune back to a framework	Early spring
H. petiolaris	No routine pruning	
Hypericum	One-third method	Spring
Ilex	Clip to shape	Spring and summer
Indigofera	Cut back to a framework	Late summer
Jasminum nudiflorum	One-third method	After flowering
J. officinale	Thin, as necessary	After flowering
Kalmia	One-third method	After flowering
Kerria	One-third method	Early summer
Kolkwitzia	One-third method	After flowering
Laurus	Clip to shape	Spring and summer
Lavandula	Trim previous year's growth	Early to mid-spring
Lavatera	Prune to a framework	Spring
Leycesteria	One-third method	After flowering
Ligustrum	Clip to shape	Spring and summer
Lonicera, climbing	Thin tangled stems	After flowering
L. shrubby	No routine pruning	
L. nitida	Clip to shape	Spring and summer
Mahonia, bushy	One-third method	Early summer

Above: *An abundance of flowers adorn this* Kalmia latifolia.

Methods of Pruning Chart

NAME OF PLANT	TYPE OF PRUNING	TIME TO PRUNE
Mahonia, groundcover	Cut to 15–30cm (6–12in) above ground level	Spring, alternate years
Mahonia, tall	Shorten flowered stems	After flowering
Olearia	One-third method	After flowering
Osmanthus	No routine pruning	
Paeonia	Cut out dead wood	Early summer
Parthenocissus	As for vines and creepers	Winter
Passiflora	Thin tangled stems	Spring
Paulownia	No pruning necessary, but can be cut back to a framework	Early spring
Perovskia	Prune to the base	Early spring
Philadelphus	One-third method	After flowering
Phlomis	Cut back side shoots	Spring
Phormium	Remove dead leaves	Late spring
Potentilla	One-third method	After flowering
Pyracantha, wall trained	Shorten side shoots	Midsummer
Ribes	One-third method	After flowering
Robinia pseudocacia	Pollarding	Late winter
Rosa	See rose section	
Rosmarinus	Clip to shape	Spring and summer
Rubus (most)	One-third method	Mid-summer

Above: *Hybrid tea roses pruned for perfect flowers.*

NAME OF PLANT	TYPE OF PRUNING	TIME TO PRUNE
R. cockburnianus,		
R. thibetanus	Cut back to ground level	Early spring
Ruta	Trim previous year's growth	Spring
Salix	No pruning necessary, but	
	some can be cut back hard	
Sambucus	One-third method,	Mid-spring
	or cut back to a framework	Early spring
Santolina	Trim previous year's growth	Mid-spring
Skimmia	No routine pruning	
Sorbaria	One-third method	Late winter to mid-spring
Spiraea, spring-flowering	One-third method	After flowering
Spiraea, summer-flowering	Trim previous year's growth	Mid-spring
Symphoricarpos	One-third method	Mid-summer
Syringa	Remove a quarter of the	
	oldest stems	Winter
Tamarix	No routine pruning	
Tilia	Pollarding	Late winter
Ulex	Clip to shape	Early summer
Viburnum	No routine pruning	
Vinca	Shear back to near ground level	Early spring
Vitis	As for vines and creepers	Winter
Weigela	One-third method	Mid-summer
Wisteria	Cut back new growth	After flowering

Above: *Radiant summer foliage of* Sambucus racemosa *'Plumosa Aurea'.*

Seasonal Pruning Chart

EARLY SPRING
Artemisia
Brachyglottis
Buddleja
Calluna
Carpenteria
Caryopteris
Ceratostigma
Chimonanthus
Colutea
Cornus alba 'Sibirica'
Cornus stolonifera
    'Flaviramea'

Corylus
Cotinus
Erica
Eucalyptus
Fuchsia (hardy)
Gaultheria
Helichrysum
Hibiscus
Hippophae
Hydrangea paniculata
Hypericum
Jasminum nudiflorum
Mahonia (tall)

Paulownia
Rubus cockburnianus
Rubus thibetanus
Salix
Sambucus
Vinca

MID-SPRING
Aucuba
Berberis (evergreen)
Buxus
Ceanothus (deciduous)
Chaenomeles
Cornus alba (most cvs)
Cotoneaster (evergreen)
Fallopia
Forsythia
Fremontodendron
Hydrangea macrophylla
Ilex
Lavandula
Ligustrum
Lonicera nitida
Mahonia (groundcover)
Phlomis
Rosmarinus
Ruta
Sambucus
Santolina
Sorbaria
Spiraea (summer-
    flowering)

Above: *A once-flowering climbing rose in bloom.*

LATE SPRING
Escallonia
Laurus
Lavatera
Passiflora
Phormium
Spiraea (spring-
    flowering)

EARLY SUMMER
Kerria
Mahonia (bushy)
Paeonia
Ulex

MIDSUMMER
Abutilon
Aucuba
Buxus

Ceanothus
Cistus
Cytisus
Deutzia
Hedera
Helianthemum
Ilex
Kalmia
Kolkwitzia
Laurus
Leycesteria
Ligustrum
Lonicera (climbing)
Lonicera nitida
Olearia
Rosmarinus
Rubus (most)
Symphoricarpos
Weigela

LATE SUMMER
Convolvulus
Daboecia
Erica
Genista
Halimiocistus
Indigofera
Jasminum officinale

WINTER
Actinidia
Berberis (deciduous)
Cotoneaster (deciduous)
Parthenocissus
Syringa
Vitis

Above: *A neatly clipped hedge.*

Above: *A healthy* pieris.

Common Names of Plants

Bay *Laurus nobilis*
Beauty bush *Kolkwitzia amabilis*
Bladder senna *Colutea*
Boston ivy *Parthenocissus tricus pidata*
Box *Buxus*
Broom *Cytisus, Genista*
Butterfly bush *Buddleja davidii*
Calico bush *Kalmia latifolia*
California lilac *Ceanothus*
Christmas box *Sarcococca*
Cinquefoil *Potentilla*
Climbing hydrangea *Hydrangea petiolaris*
Common lilac *Syringa vulgaris*
Contorted hazel *Corylus avellana 'Contorta'*
Corkscrew hazel *Corglus avellana 'Contorta'*
Cotton lavender *Santolina chamaecyparissus*
Curry plant *Helichrysum italicum*
Daisy bush *Olearia*
Dogwood *Cornus*
Dutchman's pipe *Aristolochia*
Elder *Sambucus*
False castor oil plant *Fatsia japonica*
Flowering currant *Ribes sanguineum*
Flowering quince *Chaenomeles*
Furze *Ulex*
Golden privet *Ligustrum ovalifolium 'Aureum'*
Gorse *Ulex*
Hardy plumbago *Ceratostigma willmottianum*
Harry Lauder's walking stick *Corylus avellana 'Contorta'*
Hazel *Corylus avellana*
Heather *Calluna, Daboecia, Erica*
Holly *Ilex*

Honeysuckle *Lonicera*
Indian bean tree *Catalpa bignonioides*
Ivy *Hedera*
Japanese quince *Chaenomeles*
Japonica *Chaenomeles*
Jasmine *Jasminum*
Jessamine *Jasminum*
Jew's mallow *Kerria japonica*
Kolomikta vine *Actinidia kolomikta*
Lad's love *Artemisia abrotanum*
Lavender *Lavandula*
Lemon verbena *Aloysia triphylla*
Leyland cypress *x Cupressocyparis leylandii*
Lilac *Syringa*
Mexican orange blossom *Choisya ternata*
Mile-a-minute plant *Fallopia baldschuanica*
Mock orange *Philadelphus*
Mount Etna broom *Genista aetnensis*
Moutan *Paeonia*
Old man *Artemisia abrotanum*
Ornamental vine *Vitis*
Passion flower *Passiflora caerulea*

Above: Clematis.

Peony *Paeonia*
Periwinkle *Vinca*
Portugal laurel *Prunus lusitanica*
Potato vine *Solanum crispum*
Privet *Ligustrum*
Rock rose *Cistus*
Rose of Sharon *Helianthemum, Hypericum calycinum*
Rosemary *Rosmarinus*
Rue *Ruta graveolens*
Russian sage *Perovskia atriplicifolia*
Russian vine *Fallopia baldschuanica*
Sage *Salvia officinalis*
Saint John's wort *Hypericum*
Sea buckthorn *Hippophae rhamnoides*
Silk tassel bush *Garrya elliptica*
Smoke bush *Cotinus coggygria*
Snowberry *Symphoricarpos*
Southernwood *Artemisia abrotanum*
Spanish broom *Spartium junceum*
Stag's horn sumach *Rhus typhina*
Sun rose *Cistus, Helianthemum*
Sweet bay *Laurus nobilis*
Sweet box *Sarcococca*
Torbay palm *Cordyline*
Tree peony *Paeonia*
Velvet sumach *Rhus typhina*
Virginia creeper *Parthenocissus quinquefolia*
Whitewash bramble *Rubus cockburnianus*
Willow *Salix*
Winter jasmine *Jasminum nudiflorum*
Wintersweet *Chimonanthus*
Witch hazel *Hamamelis*

Index

Abeliophyllum 54
Abutilon 54, 61
Actinidia 54, 61
Akebia 54
apples: cordons 48
    dwarf bush 46
    espaliers 47
Artemisia 54, 60
Aucuba 54, 60, 61

Berberis 44, 54, 60, 61
blackberries 52
blackcurrants 51
blueberries 53
box 42
Brachyglottis 54, 60
Buddleja 54, 60
    B. davidii 14
buds, where to cut 7
Buxus 42, 54, 60, 61

Callicarpa 54
Calluna 54, 60
Camellia 5, 54
Campsis 54
Carpenteria 54, 60
Caryopteris 54, 60
Catalpa bignonioides 54
Ceanothus 54–5, 60, 61
Cedrus atlantica 'Glauca
    Pendula' 41
Ceratostigma 55, 60
Cestrum parqui 55
Chaenomeles 37, 55, 60
Chimonanthus 55, 60
Choisya 55
Cistus 21, 55, 61
Clematis 4, 6, 30–3, 55
    C. 'Bill MacKenzie' 33
    C. 'Fireworks' 30
    C. flammula 30
    C. 'Jackmanii Superba'
    33
    C. montana 31, 57
    C.m. var. rubens
    'Continuity' 31

C. rehderiana 30
C. 'Royalty' 32
C. tibetana subsp.
    vernayi 30
Clerodendrum 55
Clethra 55
climbing plants 36
climbing roses 28, 60
clipping 17
Colutea 55, 60
conifers 40–1, 45
Convolvulus 55, 61
coppicing 12
cordons 48
Cornus alba 55, 60
    C.a. 'Sibirica' 55, 60
    C. controversa 55
    C. florida 55
    C. kousa 55
    C. stolonifera
    'Flaviramea' 55, 60
Corylopsis 55
Corylus 55, 60
Cotinus 55, 60
Cotoneaster 55, 60, 61
currants 51
cuts 7, 8
Cytisus 20, 55, 61

Daboecia 55, 61
Daphne 56
dead patches, in conifers
    41
deadheading, with shears
    16
Deutzia 56, 61
diseases 6
dogwoods 6, 12

Elaeagnus 56
Enkianthus 56
Erica 56, 60, 61
Escallonia 56, 61
espaliers 37, 47
Eucalyptus 56, 60
Euonymus 56

evergreens: clipping 17
    large-leaved 18

Fallopia 56, 60
Fatsia 56
floribunda roses 24
flowering hedges 44
foliage, grey 22
formal hedges 43
Forsythia 56, 60
Fothergilla 56
framework, cutting back
    to 14
Fremontodendron 56, 60
fruit 6—7, 46—53
Fuchsia 44, 56, 60
    F. 'Tom Thumb' 15

Garrya 56
Gaultheria 56, 60
Genista 56, 61
    G. lydia 20
gooseberries 50
grey-leaved plants 22
Griselinia 56
ground, cutting to 15

x Halimiocistus 56, 61
heathers 16
Hebe 56
Hedera 56, 61
hedge trimmers 9
hedges: formal 43
    informal flowering 44
    neglected 45
    new 42
Helianthemum 56, 61
Helichrysum 56, 60
Hibiscus 57, 60
Hippophae 57, 60
holly 18
honeysuckle 34
hybrid berries 52
hybrid tea roses 25, 58
Hydrangea macrophylla
    57, 60

Index

H. paniculata 57, 60
H. petiolaris 57
Hypericum 57, 60

Ilex 57, 60
Indigofera 57, 61
informal flowering
  hedges 44

Jasminum nudiflorum
  57, 60
  J. officinale 57, 61

Kalmia 57, 61
  K. latifolia 57
Kerria 57, 61
knives 11
Kolkwitzia 57, 61
  K. amabilis 19

Laurus 57, 61
Lavandula 57, 60
Lavatera 57, 61
leaders, removing
  competing 40
Leycesteria 57, 61
Ligustrum 57, 60, 61
  L. vulgare 17
long-handled pruners 10
Lonicera 34, 57, 61
  L. nitida 60, 61
loppers 10

Mahonia 57, 58, 60, 61

neglected hedges 45
neglected plants 23
new wood 7
  shortening 20

old wood 7
Olearia 58, 61
'one-third' method 19
Osmanthus 58

Paeonia 58, 61
Parthenocissus 58, 61
Passiflora 58, 61
Paulownia 58, 60
Perovskia 58
Philadelphus 58

Phlomis 58, 60
Phormium 58, 61
Pieris 61
pollarding 12—13
Potentilla 58
power tools 9
Pyracantha 38, 58

quinces, ornamental 37

rambling roses 7, 29
raspberries 49
redcurrants 51
rejuvenating plants 23
Ribes 58
Robinia pseudoacacia 58
Rosa
  R. 'Climbing Iceberg' 28
  R. 'Frühlingsgold' 26
  R. 'Rambling Rector' 29
  R. rugosa 44
  R. 'Savoy Hotel' 25
  R. 'Sexy Rexy' 24
roses: climbing 28, 60
  floribunda 24
  hybrid tea 25, 58
  rambling 7, 29
  shrub 4, 5, 26
  standard 27
Rosmarinus 58, 60, 61
Rubus 58, 61
  R. cockburnianus 12,
    59, 60
  R. thibetanus 59, 60
Ruta 59, 60
Salix 59, 60

S. alba vitelina
  'Britzensis' 13
Sambucus 59, 60
Santolina 59, 60
  S. chamaecyparis 22
saws 9
secateurs 10
shears 11
  deadheading with 16
shrub roses 4, 5, 26
side shoots, shortening 21
Skimmia 59
Solanum crispum
  'Glasnevin' 36
Sorbaria 59, 60
Spiraea 59, 60, 61
standard roses 27
Symphoricarpos 59, 61
Syringa 59, 61

Tamarix 59
Tilia 59
tools 9–11
topiary 17
tree pruners 11

Ulex 59, 61

Viburnum 59
Vinca 59, 60
vines 39
Vitis 59, 61
  V. coignetiae 39
  V. vinifera 'Purpurea' 39

wall-trained shrubs 37–8
Weigela 59, 61
white currants 51
willows 12
Wisteria 35, 59

yew 17, 43, 45

Above: *A floribunda rose.*